By: Mina Ibrahim

For Theo

But Theo was still asleep with his face covered in drool.

He said with his clothes on backwards and his hair in a mess.

"What's taking so long?"

Another shout came in a hurry.

Woof! He barked, and coughed up a frog.

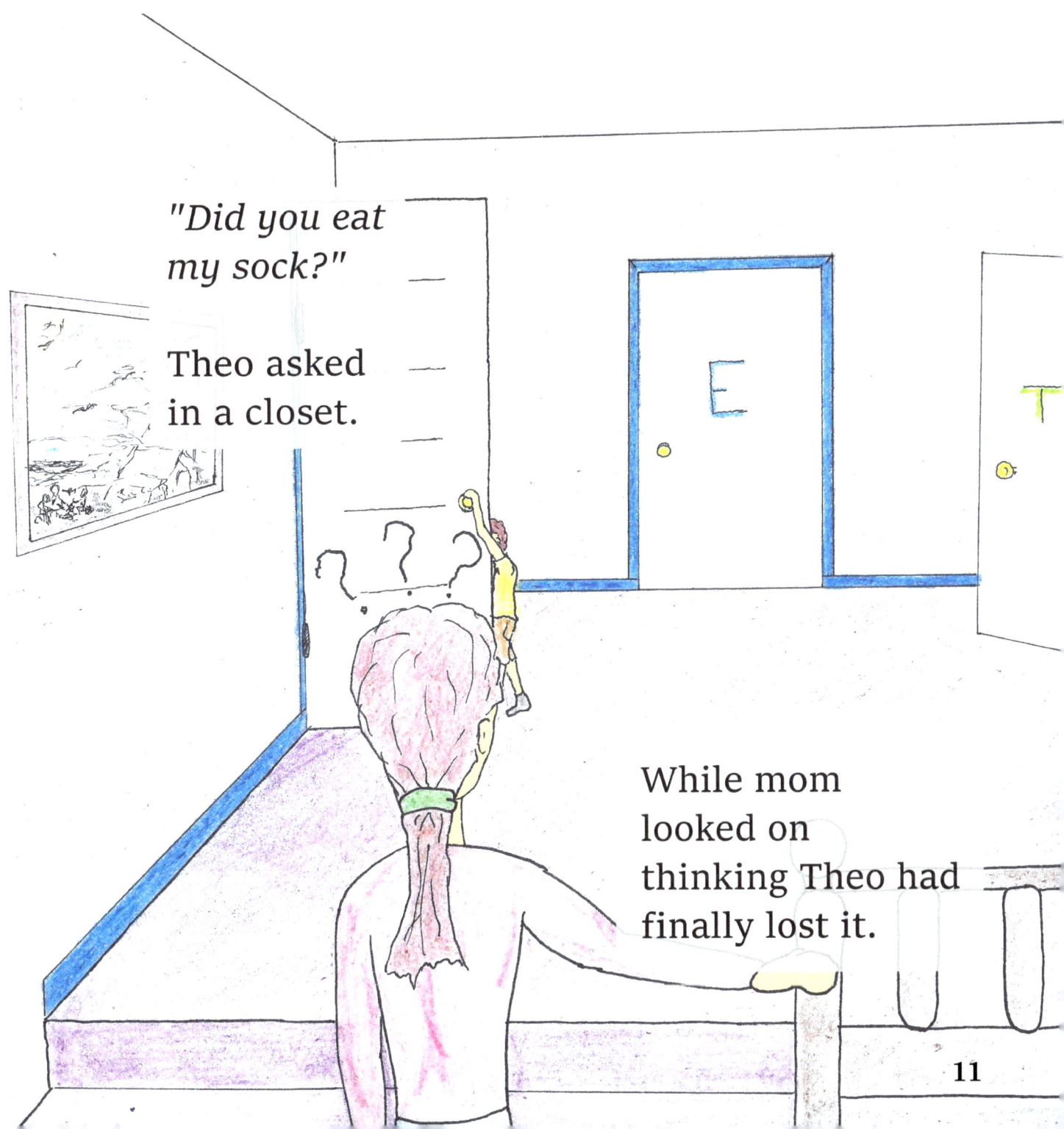

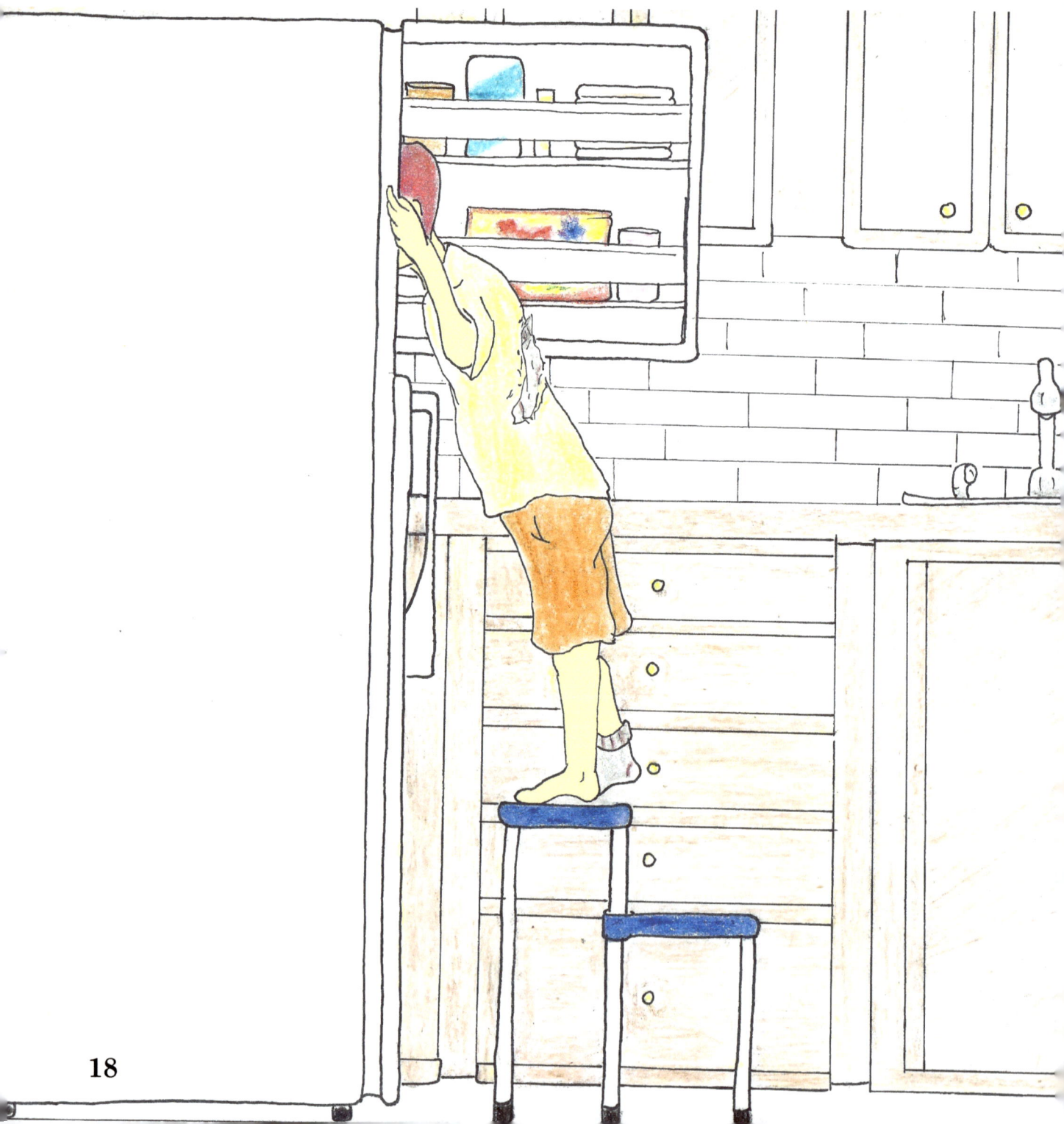

"Did you eat my sock?"

Theo asked in his neighbours garage.

Then Theo ran out the door to a school bus full of maddness.

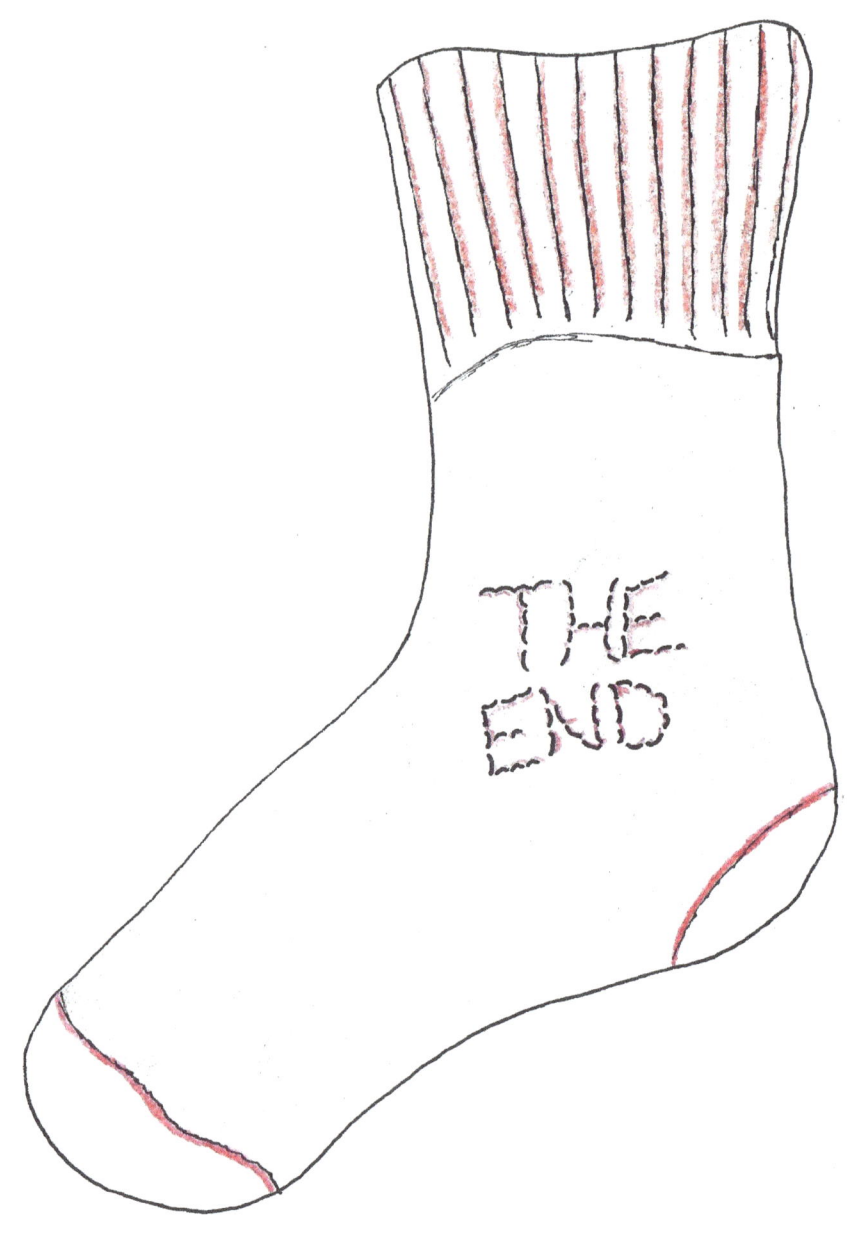

More books by Mina Ibrahim

Be Right Back gone Adulting
Moms Never Get Sick!

www.ingramcontent.com/pod-product-compliance
Lightning Source LLC
LaVergne TN
LVHW070611080526
838200LV00103B/342